Prek-3

THE KID FROM DIAMOND STREET

THE EXTRAORDINARY STORY OF BASEBALL LEGEND EDITH HOUGHTON

Written by Audrey Vernick • Illustrated by Steven Salerno

Clarion Books | Houghton Mifflin Harcourt | Boston New York

EDITH HOUGHTON used to say, "I guess I was born with a baseball in my hand," and if you'd seen little Edith playing in the 1920s, you'd probably have believed it. She was magic on the field.

Born into a Philadelphia family in 1912,
Edith was the youngest of ten kids.
Nearly as soon as she could walk,
Edith was playing ball with her
big brothers and neighbors.

baby Edith

The Houghton Family 1912
2502 Diamond Street, Philadelphia

Edith age 3

Edith age 6

Edith age 9

It didn't matter that there was no such thing as Little League. Or that most girls didn't play baseball.

If there was a sandlot game anywhere near her house on Diamond Street, you could bet she was right in the middle of it.

When she wasn't playing baseball, she was watching. From her parents' second-floor bedroom window, Edith stared out at the park across the street, where men played long summer-night games under the dim, buzzy glow of portable lights.

Edith was ten years old when she heard about the Philadelphia Bobbies, an all-female baseball team that was looking for new players. She grabbed her glove and rushed to Fairmount Park, where the Bobbies were holding tryouts.

The team was made up of older teenagers and women in their twenties, but the manager allowed Edith to try out . . . even though she was still in elementary school.

Edith was so good she made the team.

Edith was so good she was named starting shortstop.

Edith was so good she was playing professional baseball at the age of ten.

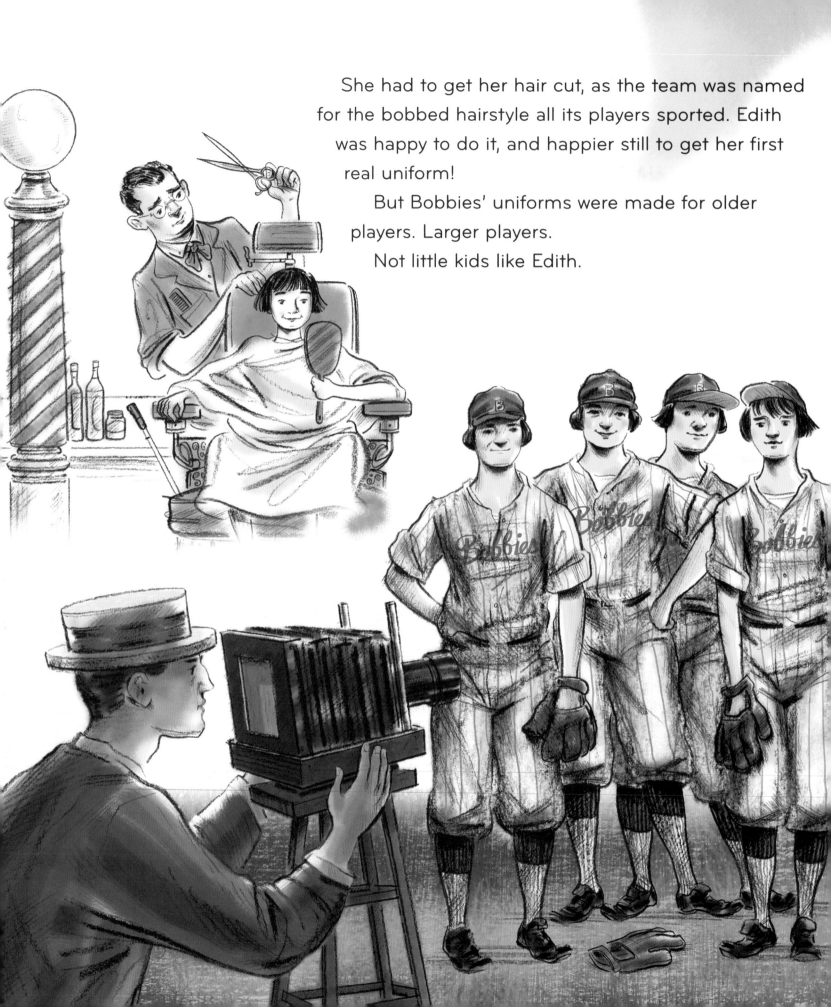

She had to get her hair cut, as the team was named for the bobbed hairstyle all its players sported. Edith was happy to do it, and happier still to get her first real uniform!

But Bobbies' uniforms were made for older players. Larger players.

Not little kids like Edith.

Her cap kept falling off until she safety-pinned it to a smaller size. Her pants fell down until she notched new holes in the belt. And her too-long sleeves kept getting in the way until she rolled them up.

She may have been the smallest one out on that field, but there was nothing puny about her skills. Newspaper reporters wrote about the incredible plays—at bat and in the field—of the girl they called "The Kid."

1922 Philadelphia Bobbies

Because they were the only female team around, the Bobbies played against men's teams all over Philadelphia, throughout Pennsylvania, and as far south as Virginia. Edith's parents came to home games whenever they could. "When my father went along, he would always be talking about how great his daughter was and all. I'd be saying, 'Pop, would you be quiet?'" But her daddy kept boasting. He clipped newspaper articles and kept a scrapbook, too.

And it wasn't only her dad who was impressed. Fans lined up to attend their games. Tickets and snacks were sold. People cheered. "I guess we were an attraction," Edith said, "being a women's team." The attention never mattered to her. The Kid just wanted to play.

Edith's parents

— include passage
about her last week

learned to
play ball with brothers did.
hit?

BOBBIES PLAYING SMART BALL
Local Girls' Team Hit Stride
EDITH HOUGHTON STARS

The Philadelphia Bobbies have struck their stride.
For the past two weeks they have won four out of five
games played, several with strong men's teams.
In play against the team from Baltimore, shortstop
Edith Houghton handled herself like a Dave Bancroft.
The ten-year-old phenom known as "The Kid" covered
the ground at shortstop and made herself a favorite
with the fans for her splendid field work and ability
at the bat. She had a clean record afield and there
can be no disputing that she is a crackerjack shortstop.
At bat she smote three safeties out of four trips to the
plate.

In 1925, when Edith was thirteen, the team had an opportunity to set forth on a great adventure. They were invited to play against male teams, mostly college-level, in Japan. The people of Japan loved baseball, and promoters were certain thousands of fans would turn out to cheer for the all-female team. JAPAN! Japan was halfway around the world!

No one Edith knew had been to Japan. Most people she knew hadn't stepped foot outside Pennsylvania.

"My parents had to go to school and explain to them about this," Edith said. "The principal and teachers agreed that I'd get more out of that trip than being in that class, and it's true."

Alaska

Canada

12 days by train

Philadelphia

Seattle

The United States

Pacific Ocean

Mexico

Hawaii

N

E

W

S

So the Kid set out on a long train journey across the country with the rest of the Bobbies. Edith was traveling without her parents, but Bobbies' manager Mary O'Gara always kept an eye out for her, making sure older players were on their best behavior around Edith and the other teenage girls.

They barnstormed through North Dakota, Montana, and Washington, playing eight exhibition games against men's teams along the way. "I didn't care who I was playing," Edith said, "as long as we were playing."

When they reached Seattle, the Bobbies got new
uniforms and equipment and boarded the *President Jefferson*,
the ship they'd take to Japan. An orchestra played and the
Bobbies threw paper streamers from the ship to the dock.
They were on their way!

At a big dance on the ship the first night, left-fielder Nettie Gans got up and played violin with the ship's orchestra.

Then the ship started rocking. A lot. Edith got really, really seasick. Just about everyone did—except for third-baseman Fereba Garnett, who kept telling her teammates to stop thinking about it. Which was impossible!

But when the sea was calm and Edith was well, she enjoyed the daily customs of the boat: removing her shoes before entering her cabin, attending dances and parties, watching movies. The Bobbies even taught the Earl of Gosford, another passenger, to dance the Charleston.

The Earl of Gosford

Best of all was taking batting
practice in the middle of the ocean!
Right there on the deck of an ocean liner
crossing the huge Pacific, the Bobbies ran drills
and honed their baseball skills under a sky of
endless blue.

When a batter really got ahold of one, it sailed
out over the rail and splashed into the dark waters
below. "We were knocking the balls out to sea,"
Edith said. (No one was rushing to make plays
against the railing—the drop down was
a big one!)

When the ship finally reached Japan, the Bobbies walked down the gangplank, grateful to be back on land. Crowds were on hand to greet them . . . reporters to interview them . . . photographers to take pictures of them!

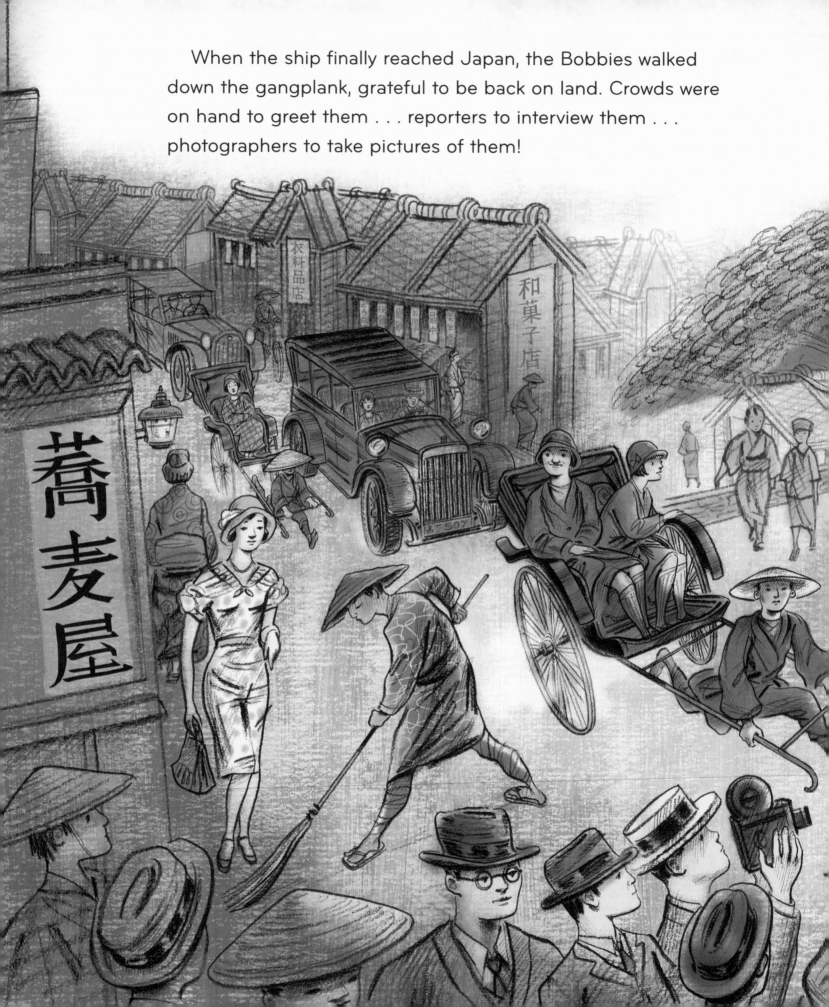

Japan was nothing like Philadelphia. The Bobbies rode on rickshaws and were surprised to see that men and women alike wore kimonos. Everything was different— even the shape of their houses!

The Bobbies' first game was in front of the biggest crowd Edith had ever played for. Tens of thousands of people watched and cheered, but it felt no different to the Kid, "because once you get out there to play, you don't see those people. You didn't even know there was anybody there. You were playing."

For the tour, a male battery (pitcher and catcher) played with the team. At first, catcher Eddie Ainsmith was concerned about the little pipsqueak at short. He worried that a girl Edith's size wouldn't be able to handle his throws to second during a steal. Like a jolly uncle, he promised Edith a yen for every catch she made. And like the pro she was, Edith nearly got rich on that deal.

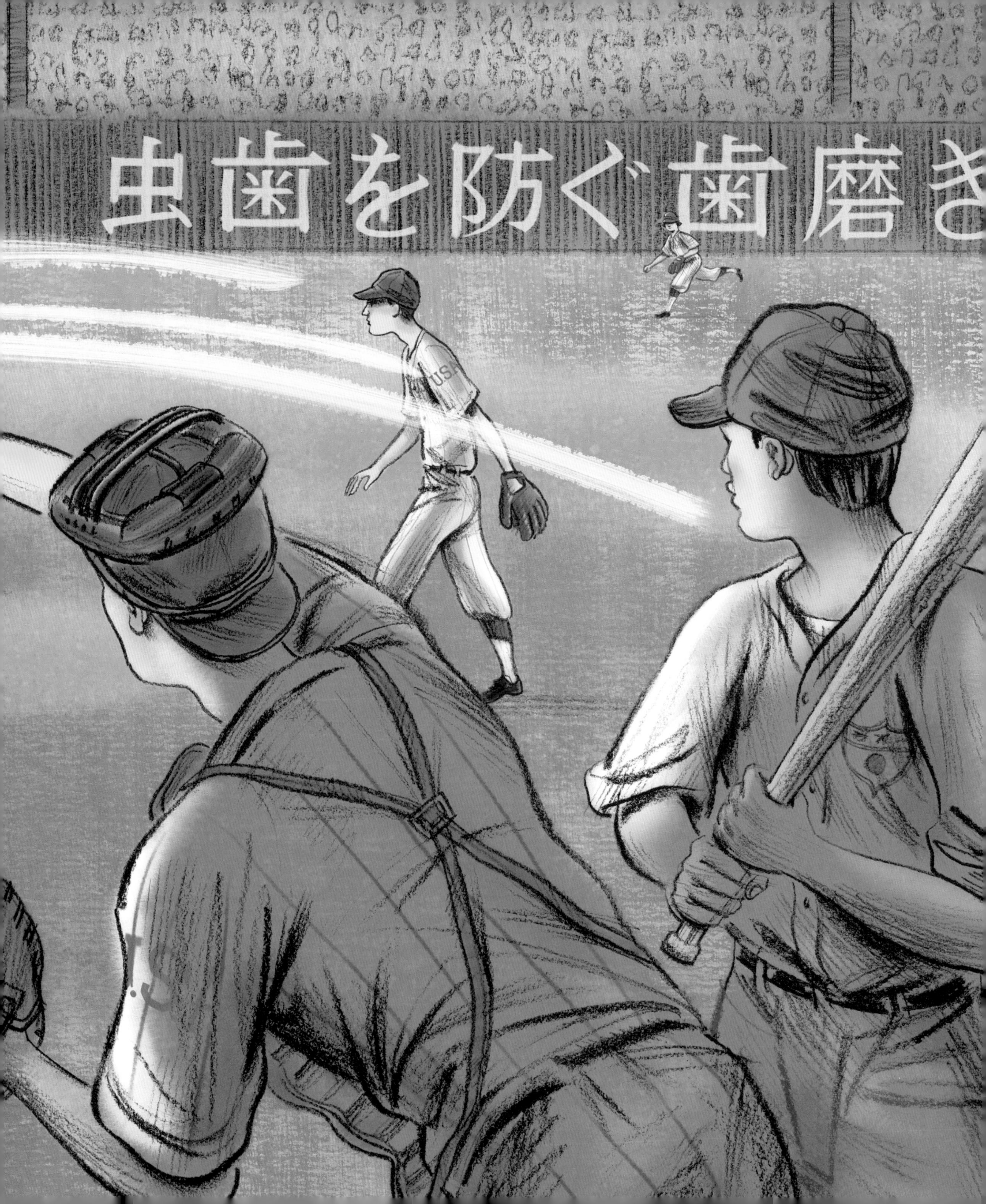
虫歯を防ぐ歯磨き
USA

Japanese newspapers reported on the crowds that came out to see the all-girl team from America. A reporter wrote that the female players "were wearing all sport shoes instead of high heels."

For two months, the Bobbies—in their sport shoes—played from city to city throughout Japan, winning more games than they lost. The Bobbies stuck together off the field too: shopping in department stores, meeting Japanese celebrities, trying to use chopsticks.

うどん

As in summer camp, the girls often sang together. Edith and Nettie sometimes played piano. Second-baseman Jenny Phillips played guitar. Nettie wrote lyrics about the Bobbies, to the tune of a popular song, "Collegiate."

"Baseball, baseball, oh we sure do love it, nothing goes above it, yeah!"
(They also tried to sing a version with what they thought were Japanese words, but it was really just a mess of goofy-sounding gibberish.)

"We were having a ball," Edith said.

But it was sometimes hard to be away from home, especially on American holidays. The night before Halloween, Edith and the Bobbies pulled together costumes and marched outside their Osaki hotel. They knew Mischief Night, as it was called back home, wasn't celebrated in Japan, but they couldn't resist. They wondered what Japanese passersby thought about their dressed-up selves, but it hardly mattered. They were together, celebrating.

When it was finally time to return home, the seas were calmer
and only one person was sick—the one who had told all
the seasick Bobbies to just think about something else.
Poor Fereba was green! They were still on the ship on
Thanksgiving, and Edith gave thanks for her wonderful
adventure and for the Bobbies, her baseball family.
After their big feast, the teammates felt so at
home that they got up to a little trouble.
The Bobbies switched up the shoes
people had left outside their cabins.
(What a surprise it must have
been to find someone
else's shoes waiting in
the morning!)

When they arrived home, they were again greeted by reporters and photographers. After posing for pictures and saying goodbye to her teammates, Edith finally returned to her family and her home on Diamond Street.

WELCOME HOME EDITH

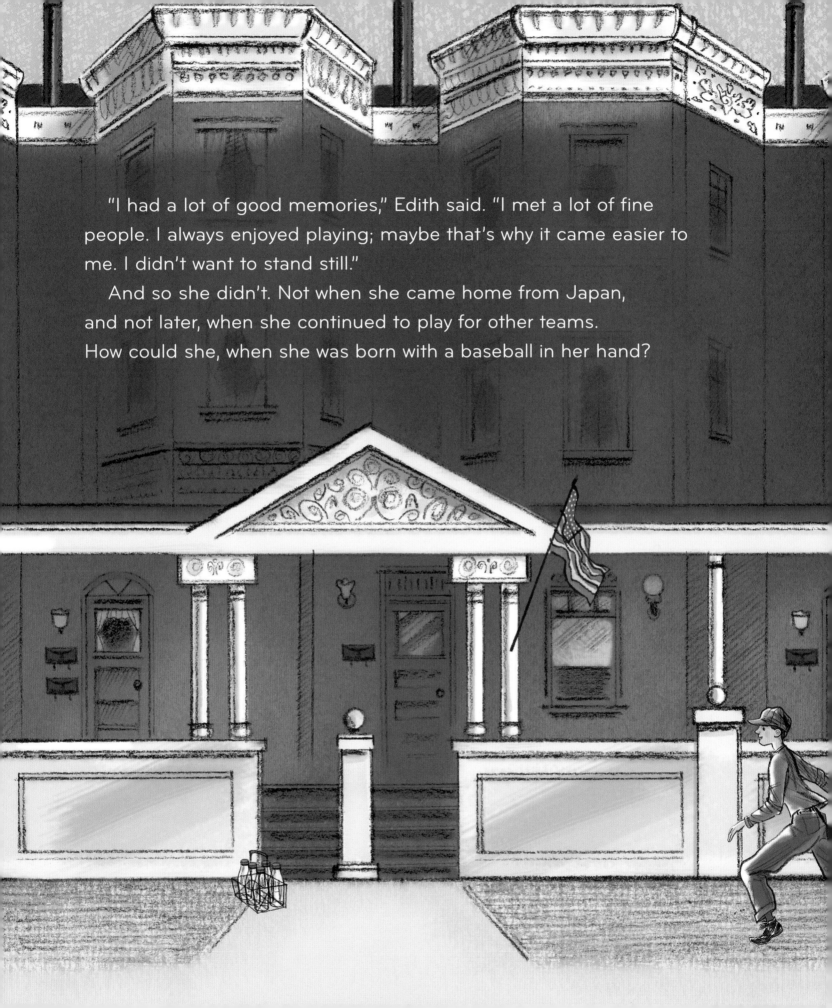

"I had a lot of good memories," Edith said. "I met a lot of fine people. I always enjoyed playing; maybe that's why it came easier to me. I didn't want to stand still."

And so she didn't. Not when she came home from Japan, and not later, when she continued to play for other teams. How could she, when she was born with a baseball in her hand?

A NOTE FROM THE AUTHOR

Edith as a Philadelphia Bobbie ◆ *Baseball Hall of Fame*

WHEN YOU CONSIDER baseball's vast history, you see thousands of amazing, impressive achievements by men. Behind that, you can see the millions of boys and men who loved the game. If you look a little harder, you'll see the women, too. As far back as the 1800s, women, wearing dresses with long, heavy skirts, were chasing down fly balls.

But baseball for women was far from commonplace. After Edith Houghton played with the Bobbies, there weren't many other teams to choose from, but Edith didn't need many. She went on to play baseball with the New York Bloomer Girls and the Boston Hollywood Girls. She would tell you she played her best ball as a member of the Hollywood Girls when she was nineteen.

After several ordinary, non-baseball jobs and serving in the WAVES (Women Accepted for Volunteer Emergency Service) during World War II, Edith felt her hand reaching for that ball again. She was hired as a Major League Scout by Philadelphia Phillies owner and president Bob Carpenter.

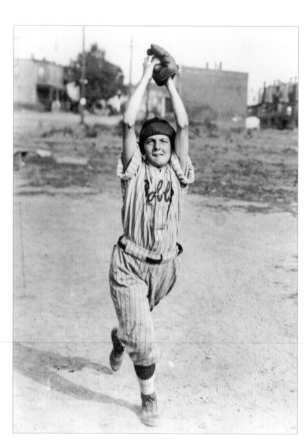

A star in the field and at the plate ◆ *Baseball Hall of Fame*

Carpenter was so impressed by Edith's knowledge and the scrapbook her father provided that he hired her despite the fact that only one other woman had ever worked as a scout. Edith scouted high school and college players for five years—traveling all over Pennsylvania and beyond.

After that, Edith's connection to baseball was primarily as a fan—watching games on TV, attending spring training near her new home in Florida. But in May 2006, she found herself honored as an important piece of its history. The Diamond Dreams Exhibit at the Baseball Hall of Fame opened on Mother's Day that year to showcase women's baseball history. There you can see the jersey Edith wore in Japan, along with the cap she wore when she was called the Kid. The Hall

As a scout for the Phillies in 1946 ◆ *Historical Society of Pennsylvania*

The Philadelphia Bobbies (Edith in front on right) ◆ *Baseball Hall of Fame*

of Fame's Research Library also has a copy of the diary Edith's teammate Nettie Gans kept during the Bobbies' tour of Japan.

When Edith Houghton died in 2013, days before her 101st birthday, articles in newspapers across the country celebrated the life she'd lived. She earned her place in baseball's rich history by living her life as a loving tribute to the sport. The joy she took in the game reminds us that baseball isn't just numbers and statistics, men and boys. Baseball is also ten-year-old girls, marching across a city to try out for a team intended for players twice their age.

Strong, determined, fierce, a standout on the field:
Anna, this one had to be for you.
—A. V.

To my big brother, Joe, who missed going to Fenway
for the very first time because of the measles!
—S.S.

◆ ◆ ◆ **ACKNOWLEDGMENTS** ◆ ◆ ◆

Thanks to Tim Wiles, who, in his former role as Director of Research at the National Baseball Hall of Fame, brought the Bobbies to my attention. Sadly, I learned of their existence very near the end of Edith Houghton's long life, and my attempts to contact her went unanswered. Thanks also to Jenny Ambrose at the Baseball Hall of Fame.

Clarion Books • 3 Park Avenue, New York, New York 10016 • Text copyright © 2016 by Audrey Vernick • Illustrations copyright © 2016 by Steven Salerno • All rights reserved. For information about permission to reproduce selections from this book, write to trade.permissions@hmhco.com or to Permissions, Houghton Mifflin Harcourt Publishing Company, 3 Park Avenue, 19th Floor, New York, New York 10016. • Clarion Books is an imprint of Houghton Mifflin Harcourt Publishing Company. • www.hmhco.com • The illustrations for this book were created with charcoal, ink, and gouache, with added digital color rendered in Adobe Photoshop. • The text was set in Bryant • Library of Congress Cataloging-in-Publication Data • Names: Vernick, Audrey. | Salerno, Steven, illustrator. • Title: The kid from Diamond Street : the extraordinary story of baseball legend Edith Houghton / Audrey Vernick ; illustrated by Steven Salerno. • Description: New York, New York : Clarion Books, 2016. • Identifiers: LCCN 2015015724 | ISBN 9780544611634 (hardback) • Subjects: LCSH: Houghton, Edith, 1912-2013. | Baseball players—United States—Biography. | Women baseball players—United States—Biography. | BISAC: JUVENILE NONFICTION / Biography & Autobiography / Sports & Recreation. | JUVENILE NONFICTION / Sports & Recreation / Baseball & Softball. | JUVENILE NONFICTION / Girls & Women. | JUVENILE NONFICTION / Biography & Autobiography / Women. | JUVENILE NONFICTION / History / United States / 20th Century. • Classification: LCC GV865.H636 V47 2016 | DDC 796.357092—dc23
LC record available at http://lccn.loc.gov/2015015724
Manufactured in Malaysia • TWP 10 9 8 7 6 5 4 3 2 1
4500561097